The TIME

trekkers

visit the

ROMANS

ANTONY MASON

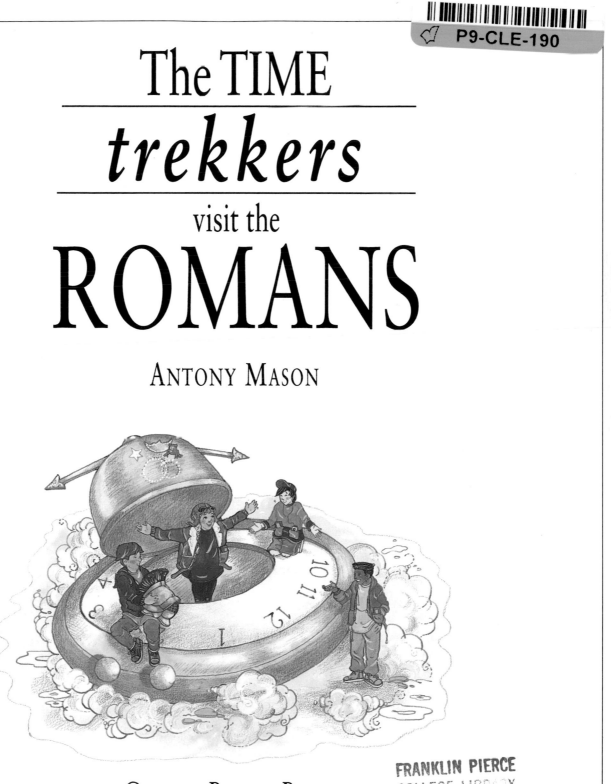

COPPER BEECH BOOKS

BROOKFIELD, CONNECTICUT

© Aladdin Books Ltd 1995

Designed and produced by
Aladdin Books Ltd
28 Percy Street
London W1P 0LD

First published in
the United States in 1995 by
Copper Beech Books, an imprint of
The Millbrook Press
2 Old New Milford Road
Brookfield, Connecticut 06804

Editor
Jim Pipe
Designed by
David West Children's Book Design
Designer Simon Morse
Picture Research
Brooks Krikler Research
Illustrated by Sheena Vickers &
Dave Burroughs

Printed in Belgium

Library of Congress Cataloging-in-
Publication Data
Mason, Antony.
The Romans / by Antony Mason :
illustrated by Sheena Vickers and
Dave Burroughs.
p. cm. -- (The time trekkers visit the --)
Includes index.
Added title page title: Time trekkers
visit the Romans.
ISBN 1-56294-910-1 (lib. bdg.). --
ISBN 1-56294-936-5 (pbk.)
1. Rome--Civilization--Juvenile
literature. [1. Rome--Civilization.] I.
Vickers, Sheena, ill. II. Burroughs,
Dave, ill. III. Title. IV. Title: Time
trekkers visit the Romans V. Series.
DG77.M37 1995   95-13711
937--dc20   CIP AC

INTRODUCTION
The Time trekkers

The Time trekkers are Lucy, Jools, Eddie, and Sam. Using the time machine invented by Lucy's eccentric grandfather, they travel through time and space on amazing voyages of discovery. Their gizmos are always ready to answer any questions!

But before we follow their journey back to the world of ancient Rome, let's meet the four adventurers...

Lucy – As the oldest of the four, Lucy can get a bit bossy. But when the going gets tough, the others rely on her to save the day.

Jools – He's always in a rush, but when he does stop, he usually gets caught up in the local wildlife. Look out for his pet frog, Kevin.

Eddie – With his knowledge of history, it's Eddie's job to set the controls on the time machine. But he does have a tendency to drift off into a dreamworld of his own!

Sam – When the time machine starts acting up, call Sam, the Time trekkers' research scientist. She's a whiz with gizmos and all kinds of gadgets, but sometimes gets so wrapped up in her portable stereo, she doesn't notice the danger around her!

The Gizmo

To use the gizmo, simply read the Time trekkers' question bubbles, then look to the gizmo for the answer! The gizmo has three subject buttons:

- 🔍 *Science (Orange)*
- ⊕ *Places and People (Purple)*
- 🕐 *History and Arts (Red)*

And two extra special functions:

- 💀 *X ray (Yellow)*
- **T** *Translator (Blue)*

AQUEDUCT

It's an aqueduct – a bridge for water! Its sloping channels carry fresh water across valleys and into the city.

DRAINS

water flows into drain

Roman drains help to prevent floods and remove dirty water from the city streets.

Subject logo

Gizmo's answer

Control panels

It was Sunday afternoon, and everyone was bored – everyone but Lucy, who was reading a book about the Roman Emperors. "Why are you so interested in the Romans?" asked Jools. "Everything I've heard about them makes them sound just like us."

"I know they didn't have electricity," said Sam.

"Why would that make much difference?"

"Well," said Lucy, "There's only one way to find out."

TIME SCALE

Though the Roman Empire ended around 1,500 years ago, you'll have to go back 1,900 years to see it at its most powerful.

1990s	NOW!
1885	Invention of the automobile.
1776	United States gains independence.
1653	Taj Mahal completed in India.
1492	Columbus reaches the Americas.
1066	Normans conquer England.
570	Birth of prophet Mohammed.
476	Final collapse of Roman Empire.
44 BC	Death of Julius Caesar, the greatest Roman leader.
753 BC	Founding of Rome.

How far back in time do we have to go to see the Romans?

"What do you think?" shouted Eddie. "Shall we go for 1,900 years ago?" They all agreed. Eddie set the dials. *Time: Minus 1,900. Destination: Rome.* Go! The green light flickered twice, then Whooosh...!

The adventurers heard the deep roar of time racing backward, and felt a peculiar, almost sickening spinning sensation. Suddenly, the spinning stopped. Only now they heard another roar: the deafening roar of a crowd. They had landed in the middle of a chariot race!

What on earth is this place?

ROME: CIRCUS MAXIMUS

You're in Rome, the capital of the Roman Empire, a city of about 1,000,000 people. Romans get their name from this city, though not all Romans come from Rome. Your precise location is Circus Maximus. This is the largest arena in the city, built especially for chariot racing. Chariot racing is one of the Romans' favorite sports.

The chariot race soon came to its dramatic finish. The Time trekkers were carried away by the excitement of it all. They shouted and cheered with the rest of the crowd when the winner received his crown.

Afterward, they followed the crowd into the streets of Rome. Before long, they found themselves in the center of the city, in a large square decorated with statues and monuments, and surrounded by very grand buildings and temples.

> What is this place?

> What is that man saying? What language is he speaking?

> Brevis esse laboro, obscurus fio.

LATIN

He is a politician, and he is saying, "I strive to be brief, and I become obscure." In other words, by trying to make his speech short, he makes it harder to understand!

He is speaking in Latin, the language of the Romans. English and other European languages like French and Spanish contain a large number of words that originally come from Latin. Look at the politician's words:

- from *brevis* we get "brief"
- from *laboro* we get "labor"
- from *obscurus* we get "obscure"

THE FORUM OF ROME

You are at the heart of the capital. Every Roman town had a forum. Originally it was the marketplace, and also the main meeting place. But over the years, the Forum of Rome turned into a center for law and religion, and the market stalls were moved away. The grand buildings around you are temples, monuments, and basilicas or halls where large meetings are held. The statues are of great leaders and generals.

The Time trekkers wandered on through the city, and soon found themselves on a busy main street, lined with shops and workshops. At first, everything seemed very different from their local shops! The shops had no glass windows, and there was no traffic (carts weren't allowed on the streets during the day). Once they had walked around, some shops did look familiar: the butcher's, the pharmacy, and the shoe store.

"Ave!" – Jools heard someone calling. He looked up and there was a boy waving to him.

What kind of money do the Romans have?

He says that this silk comes all the way from the Far East. Can that be true?

ROMAN TRADE

Yes. Though Romans have never been to China, their huge empire (covering most of Europe and all the countries around the Mediterranean Sea) gives them the power and contacts to buy goods from the other side of the world.

ROMAN EMPIRE
117 AD

MEDICINE

Some Romans still prefer to cure their illness by making offerings to the gods, often with a charm shaped like the part of the body which is in pain (right). But most go to doctors who use medicines made from a wide variety of herbs and other plants, such as rosemary, sage (left), and garlic (right). The patient often buys them from a pharmacy, like this one.

ROMAN MONEY

The Romans use coins. (Paper money will be invented by the Chinese in another 1,000 years or so!) The first Roman coins were made of bronze. The lighter the coin, the less it was worth.

Later, they made more valuable coins in silver (called *denarii*) and gold (called *aurei*). Julius Caesar was the first leader to put his portrait on coins.

Is this stuff medicine?

The boy who had waved to Jools was called Cassio. He had easily spotted the adventurers who, instead of the usual togas, wore the strangest clothes. He was delighted to make some new friends, and invited them back to his home.

It was clear that Cassio's parents were wealthy Roman citizens, for they lived in a very grand house. Then, when Cassio asked the adventurers to supper, it turned out to be a Roman feast!

What are they eating?

ROMAN FOOD

Wealthy Romans eat a large variety of foods, such as seafood (*below*), poultry, meat stews, beans, lettuce, fruit, nuts, dates, and even more unusual dishes like stuffed dormice (*above*). The Romans have not heard of potatoes, tomatoes, coffee, or tea, however. Their main drink is wine. Many recipes are very spicy and served with a fish sauce called *garum*. At a feast, Romans eat while lying on couches.

CITIZENS AND SLAVES

No. Only the aristocratic "patricians," the rich and the powerful, live like this. Most ordinary citizens (called *plebeians*) and non-citizens live simple lives. The large number of slaves in Rome have no freedom and usually spend their lives working for patricians.

Patrician

Plebeian

Non-citizen

Slave

This is wonderful! Do all the Romans live as well as this?
I like the music! What kind of instruments do the Romans have?
MUSICAL INSTRUMENTS
Music was played to guests during dinner parties, and also at games, theaters, and religious ceremonies.
The musicians were usually slaves or freedmen (freed slaves). Common instruments included pipes, flutes, brass horns, rattles, and cymbals.
Harp
Flute
Drum
Cymbal

The next day Cassio planned to take Eddie and Jools to the public baths. But Jools had gone off for a walk! By the time he arrived back, Cassio and Eddie were nowhere to be found. "I know," thought Jools. "I can use the X ray on my Gizmo to see if they've gone in already."

Looking down, he spotted the girls at the door of the baths: What were they waiting for?

Isn't there any soap?

Why aren't we allowed in?

The women's session is 11am to 1pm

SWEATING AND SCRAPING

Soap (a mixture of animal fat and wood ash) is used by the Celts, but the Romans think it is very uncivilized!

Instead, the Romans sit in a steam bath, then rub olive oil (from a flask, right) onto their bodies.

They scrape away the oil and dirt with a curved blade called a *strigil*. So scrape yourself, Eddie, then ask Cassio to do your back!

Strigils

Returning to the house, the trekkers collapsed in Cassio's yard, exhausted by the hot summer sun. "I think I'm going to melt," moaned Eddie. "In that case," said Cassio, "why don't we all go to my villa in the hills? It's much cooler there."

The next day, even Eddie was up in time for the long journey to the country. As they reached the border of the city, they passed some builders at work. "Wow!" said Sam. "Look how they put up such enormous buildings without even using machines."

What's that bridge?

Why are Roman roads so good?

ROMAN ROADS

smooth stone
stone/cement layers
drain
sand

High-quality roads allow Roman troops to move rapidly around the empire.

CONCRETE

The Romans started using concrete (a mix of gravel, sand, and cement) in about 100 AD. To build walls, they pour it into the gap between two rows of bricks.

AQUEDUCT

It's an aqueduct – a bridge for water! Its sloping channels carry fresh water across valleys and into the city.

DRAINS

water flows into drain

Roman drains help to prevent floods and remove dirty water from the city streets.

"Ouch," said Lucy, getting out of the cart. "Those wooden wheels weren't built for comfort. I won't be able to sit down for a week." But away from the heat and noise of the city, Lucy and the others soon forgot about their tiring journey. Staying at the villa felt like a real vacation: the Time trekkers could walk in the gardens and play in the fountains.

They also visited neighboring farms, collecting chickens' eggs for supper, and even riding horses. Cassio showed them how to use a sword. "I don't think we'll need to know how to use one," joked Eddie. But then...

Those people seem to be doing all the hard work!

SLAVERY

There are thousands of slaves (men and women) in the Roman Empire. Most were captured in wars, and many are very skilled. They are sold at slave markets, and some wear identification tags (above).

Some owners treat their slaves well and even grant them freedom. But for most, life is hard, and many are treated cruelly.

TENEMENE
FVGIA·ET·REVO
GAMENDDOMNVM
EVVIVENTIVMI·IN
KRACALLISTI

FARM ANIMALS

The earth in the fields is broken up and turned over each year by plows, usually pulled by a pair of oxen. Though the oxen are strong, plowing is still hard work.

Harvesting equipment is pushed along by oxen or donkeys. It is used to cut the wheat stalks and collect the grain.

Disaster struck! Out for a walk, Eddie and Sam got hopelessly lost. Shortly after, they were stopped by a group of soldiers, who asked where they were from. How could they explain? The soldiers thought they were probably escaped slaves. Sam and Eddie were arrested, taken to Rome, and sold in the slave market.

They were bought by a trader who planned to take them to Africa. While he prepared for the voyage, he made Sam and Eddie load sacks onto the ship!

WARSHIPS

The oars each weigh over 23 pounds (10 kg)!

The ship without sails is a warship. It is called a *quinquereme* because *quinque* means five in Latin, and the rowers are grouped in fives (on three layers, *above*). With 300 rowers, these ships can move very swiftly. On the front is a sharp ram, which is used to make a hole in enemy ships. The ship carries about 120 troops.

21

The ship took Sam and Eddie to North Africa, where they became slaves to the governor. He was the Roman in charge of the province, and he lived in great luxury. But trouble was brewing. The local people were in revolt and had taken over one of the nearby towns.

To bring the rebels under control, the governor marched out with his army, and Sam and Eddie went with him. Arriving at the siege, they tried to help him put on his armor – without much success!

The Romans look really organized.

How do they attack the town?

Just how much armor do you need?

Can't you tie that lace properly? I'm selling you as soon as I get to Rome.

LEGIONARY ARMOR

metal helmet

cooking pan and dishes

javelin

body armor

sword

tools for digging ditches and earthworks

wooden shield

sandals with metal studs

A legionary (a foot soldier in a legion) has to carry his body armor, shield, and weapons, as well as a heavy backpack.

THE LEGION

cohort 1 2 3 4 5 6 7 8 9 10

century

The Roman army is very well organized. Each legion of 5,000 men is divided into groups of 100 men called centuries. Each century is led by a centurion. Six centuries make up a cohort, except for the first cohort, which has ten centuries.

SAFETY IN ATTACK

Attacking the walls, legionaries cluster together to form a shell with their shields.

ARTILLERY

In sieges (attacks on towns), the Romans use catapults built like huge wooden crossbows to fire spearlike missiles. They also use great slings to hurl giant rocks at the enemy.

23

Back in Italy, Lucy and Jools were very worried. What had become of their friends? It was a complete mystery. Cassio's family could offer no explanation, either. Lucy and Jools decided to travel back to Rome to see if there was any news of them there.

After a month, they had still heard nothing. Not even the time machine could figure out where Sam and Eddie had gone. Cassio's father suggested that they all go to a temple to pray to the gods, to make an offering, and perhaps consult an augur.

They went to the temple of Minerva, one of the many gods worshipped by the Romans.

> What does augur mean?

> How many gods do the Romans believe in?

ROMAN GODS & GODDESSES

Jupiter chief of the gods

Vesta goddess of sacred fire

Mars god of war

Minerva goddess of wisdom

Mercury messenger of the gods

Venus goddess of love

AUGURS

The Romans believe that certain people can tell the future and explain what is happening far away. To do this, they look for various signs.

Augurs look at the flight path of birds (*top*), the pattern of lightning, or even the way chickens feed, to search for messages from the gods. *Haruspices* study the innards of animals (like sheep) sacrificed to the gods, to try to see the future.

The augur said that Sam and Eddie faced great danger. That worried Lucy and Jools even more! To take their minds off their worries, Cassio took Lucy and Jools to see a gladiator fight in the Colosseum.

Two small gladiators faced two enormous gladiators – two mighty champions! The crowd roared and cheered, then fell silent. Suddenly, Jools and Lucy recognized Sam and Eddie. They had been sold to the gladiator school!

"Tell the others to meet us by the time machine," Lucy said to Jools, "I've got an idea." Two minutes passed, and nothing happened. What was Lucy up to? Jools and Cassio shouted to the others as the gladiators attacked.

As if by magic, the gladiators stopped dead in their tracks. Something growled behind them. Lucy had opened the door to the lion cage!

EDDIE!

SAM!

GLADIATORS

Yes! Gladiators are usually slaves or prisoners, so they must fight. They are armed with either shields and swords, or tridents and nets. Sometimes they fight wild animals, such as lions or bears. Fights are to the death, but a gladiator can appeal for mercy. If the crowd thinks he has fought badly, an official gives the thumbs-down signal and he dies.

death

life

THE COLOSSEUM

The Colosseum (*above*) is the greatest amphitheater in the Empire, holding over 50,000 people – so there are lots of ways out! As well as staging gladiator fights, the Colosseum is flooded to stage sea-battles, sometimes with live crocodiles!

As the gladiators turned to face the lions, Eddie and Sam raced for the exit. Within minutes, the Time trekkers were together again in the safety of the time machine. "Thanks for everything, Cassio, but we'd better go," shouted Eddie as he tapped on the controls. "Let's see, 300 years should be enough."

It wasn't. They landed in the middle of an invasion! Wild horsemen charged through the streets of Rome, burning buildings, knocking over statues, and stealing treasures.

What's going on?

I guess this spells the end of Rome!

THE BARBARIANS

Hun   Visigoth   Vandal

It's A.D. 410 and the Visigoths are attacking Rome. After this, the Empire falls apart. Soon the Vandals will attack Gaul, and in 451, Attila leads the Huns to the gates of Rome, which collapses in 476.

THE BYZANTINE EMPIRE

Since A.D. 395, the Empire has actually been split into two: one half of it based on the old Greek city, Byzantium, which has been renamed Constantinople.

This Christian empire will survive the Barbarian invasions and develop into the powerful Byzantine Empire. This lasts for 1,000 years until its conquest by the Turks in 1453. They rename the city Istanbul.

29

This time, Jools tapped on the time machine, desperately pressing the button marked PRESENT. In no time at all, the Time trekkers were whisked back to the present, where they landed in someone's front yard. Phew! Safe at last! As they looked around them, they thought about their amazing adventure.

The Romans were so different in many ways: Think of the Roman gods, the slaves, the togas, and the gladiators. But, in many ways, they were just the same.

THE GIZMO PUZZLER — SEE HOW WELL YOU DO!

1. Lucy visited all sorts of buildings on the adventure. Which ones do we still have today? (Hint: the pharmacy on page 11 is one example.)

2. Jools is holding some Roman coins which he brought back with him. How many other objects did you spot that we use just like the Romans?

3. Though the Romans didn't have cars or electricity, Sam noticed some devices they used to help them. What are they?

4. Can you find Jools's frog, Kevin?

THE ANSWERS — JUST TURN THE BOOK UPSIDE DOWN AND LOOK AT IT IN A MIRROR!